EXPERIENCING
THE TRINITY

EXPERIENCING THE TRINITY

DARRELL W. JOHNSON

REGENT COLLEGE PUBLISHING
• Vancouver, British Columbia •

Experiencing the Trinity
Copyright ©2002 by Darrell W. Johnson

Published 2002 by Regent College Publishing
5800 University Boulevard, Vancouver, BC V6T 2E4 Canada
www.regentpublishing.com

Experiencing the Trinity was first delivered as a series of sermons entitled "At the
Center of the Universe is a Relationship" to the congregation of Glendale
Presbyterian Church, Glendale, California, in the summer of 1998.

Views expressed in works published by Regent College Publishing are those of the
author and do not necessarily represent the official position of Regent College.

Unless otherwise noted, Scripture quotations are from the New International
Version of the Bible, copyright ©1973, 1978 by the International Bible Society.
Used by permission of Zondervan Publishers.

National Library of Canada Cataloguing in Publication Data

Johnson, Darrell W., 1947-
  Experiencing the Trinity

  Includes bibliographical references.
  ISBN 1-55361-027-X (Canada)
  ISBN 1-57383-216-2 (United States)

  1. Trinity. 2. Apologetics. I. Title.
BT111.3.J63 2002   231'.044   C2002-910506-1   v.3

For Sharon

*You implicitly live the reality
which I seek to articulate.
One day I will catch up with you.*

Holy, holy, holy! Lord God Almighty!
Early in the morning our song shall rise to Thee;
Holy, holy, holy, merciful and mighty!
God in three Persons, blessed Trinity!

Holy, holy, holy! All the saints adore Thee,
Casting down their golden crowns around the glassy sea;
Cherubim and seraphim falling down before Thee,
Who was, and is, and evermore shall be.

—Reginald Heber, 1826

CONTENTS

-1-

FINDING
THE TRINITY

Following the "simple Jesus"

For many people the doctrine of the Trinity is nothing but a hopeless puzzle, the pieces of which simply do not fit. Three is not one and one is not three, no matter how you figure it. Even among some church-goers the doctrine sometimes considered an intellectual embarrassment, a part of the Christian faith that should be relegated to a by-gone era.[1] No wonder that many of our Jewish and Muslim friends have concluded that, when it all boils down, Christians believe in three gods, not one.

Certainly the doctrine of the Trinity isn't simple. Thomas Jefferson probably expressed the frustrated sentiments of many when he suggested that the doctrine should be abandoned all together:

> When we shall have done away with the incomprehensible jargon of the Trinitarian arithmetic, that three are one, and one is three; when we shall have knocked down the artificial scaffolding reared to mask from view the simple

13

structure of Jesus; when, in short, we shall have unlearned everything which has been taught since his day, and get back to the pure and simple doctrines he inculcated, we shall then be truly and worthily his disciples.[2]

Do away with the "incomprehensible jargon" of Trinitarian arithmetic, suggests Jefferson. Get back to the simple fact of Jesus, and away from all that philosophical mumble-jumble. Jefferson's advice to focus on the pure and simple truths he taught and observed is appealing.

I believe that Thomas Jefferson was part right and part wrong. He was correct in the sense that Christians need to focus on Jesus more, but he was mistaken in thinking that this would get us back to "simple" doctrines and away from the doctrine of the Trinity. The irony is that when we follow Jefferson's advice, we end up at the feet of the Triune God. Or, to put it another way, it is precisely when we do focus on the simple facts of Jesus that we find ourselves drawn into theological grappling which keeps ending up at the doctrine of the Trinity.

We should not be surprised. That is how the doctrine of the Trinity came about in the first place—not by aimless philosophical speculation, but through the early church's experience of the resurrected Christ:

> Then the eleven disciples went to Galilee, to the mountain where Jesus had told them to go. When they saw him, they worshipped; but some doubted. Then Jesus came to them and said, "All authority in heaven and on earth has been given to me. Therefore go and make disciplines of all nations, baptizing them in the name of the Father and of

the Son and of the Holy Spirit, and teaching them to obey everything I have commanded you. And surely I am with you always, to the very end of the age."

Matthew 28:16-20

It was the "simple Jesus" himself who said that "all authority in heaven and on earth" had been given to him. And it was the "simple Jesus" who said "Lo, I am with you always even to the end of the age." While it might not be obvious to us today, Jesus' words would have brought back a powerful image in the minds of his disciples. "The Lord himself goes before you and will be with you; he will never leave you nor forsake you"—these are the words the living God spoke to Moses as Israel left Egypt to cross the desert (Deut. 31:8). Just as God sent Moses to lead the Israelites out of Egypt, Jesus sends out his disciples to lead a new exodus out of spiritual slavery. The parallels here are remarkable. Christ echoes the very words of God to the Israelites, promising his eternal presence and power (see also Exod. 4:12-13; 33:14-17).

And notice how Jesus' own disciples responded in their encounter with Jesus immediately after the resurrection: "When they saw him, they worshipped him." Those who knew Jesus best *worshipped him*. These were not ivory tower theologians, but everyday people who experienced the power of God in the risen Christ. Buddha would have rebuked his followers for such an act of adoration. So would Moses, Socrates, Confucius and certainly Muhammad. Why didn't Jesus rebuke his disciples?

Instead, Jesus says, "Go, make disciples of all nations,

15

baptizing them in the name of the Father and of the Son and of the Holy Spirit." Note his exact words—"baptizing them in *the* name,"—singular. This singular name inculcates, to use Thomas Jefferson's term, a "three-fold-ness." Jesus is saying that the living God has a new name: "Father, Son and Holy Spirit."

So let's knock down the Trinitarian scaffolding for a moment. Let's hear Jesus speak in his own words:

> "All things have been handed over to me by my Father; and no one knows the Son except the Father; nor does anyone know the Father, except the Son, and anyone to whom the Son wills to reveal him."
>
> Matthew 11:27

> "I and the Father are One."
>
> John 10:30

> "He who has seen me has seen the Father."
>
> John 14:9

> "I will ask the Father, and he will give you another Paraclete (Helper), that he may be with you forever, that is the Spirit of Truth, whom the world cannot receive, because it does not behold him or know him, but you know him since he abides with you and will abide in you."
>
> John 14:16-17

> "These things I have spoken to you, while abiding with you. But the Paraclete (Helper), the Holy Spirit, whom the Father will send in my name, he will teach you all

things and bring to your remembrance all that I said to
you."

John 14:26

"When the Paraclete comes, whom I will send to you from
the Father, that is the Spirit of truth, who proceeds from the
Father, he will bear witness of me."

John 15:26

"If anyone loves me, they will keep my word; and the
Father and I will love them, and we will come to them and
make our home with them."

John 14:23

Few would accuse Jesus of Nazareth of speaking
philosophical mumble-jumble. Even non-Christians will
often say that he is a great teacher, if not the greatest teacher
in history. But, as we have just read, the "simple" teaching
teachings of Jesus raise many complicated questions. Who
is this Father whom Jesus claims to reveal? And how is
Jesus related to this Father? In what sense are they one?
Who is this Holy Spirit whom Jesus promises to send from
the Father and whom the Father sends in Jesus' name?
Who is the "we" who through the presence of the Paraclete
takes up residence in the lives of Jesus' disciples?

When we go back to the simple Jesus, we hear him speak
of a living God who in some way exists in some sort of
three-fold-ness.

Moreover, we move out of Christian circles and present
the "simple Jesus," before we know it we begin to use
Trinitarian language and concepts.

Lesslie Newbigin, the late Anglican missionary to India, argued that there is simply no way to preach Jesus without reference to the Trinity.[3] "How does one say who Jesus is in a pagan situation?" Newbigin asked. "Presumably the hearers have already heard the word 'god' in their vocabulary. How is the name of Jesus to be related henceforth in their minds to that word?" Is Jesus another God? Newbigin came to the following conclusion:

> The truth is one cannot preach Jesus even in the simplest terms without preaching him as the Son. His revelation of God is the revelation of 'an only begotten from the Father', and you cannot preach him without speaking of the Father and the Son.

And how does one speak of Jesus being present with us without speaking of the Holy Spirit? Even the most elementary preaching of the Gospel raises issues which led the church in the direction of the doctrine of the Trinity.

This controversial, mind-stretching doctrine we call "the Trinity" did not emerge out of an ivory tower think-tank. It emerged out of the life and mission of ordinary Christian congregations. Yes, the "church fathers," as they are called, employed the philosophical language and concepts of their own day. But they were not engaged in the task for the sake of mere speculation. They were pastors and elders seeking to faithfully present Jesus Christ. They were deacons and small group leaders seeking to lead their flocks into the fullness of life in Jesus. They wanted to worship and pray in ways worthy of the living God whom they had come to know in

Jesus. Those who shaped the doctrine of the Trinity were ordinary disciples of Jesus attempting to understand and proclaim his Gospel. They ended up where they did because of concrete issues of life and faith—which might warn us that rightly understanding the Trinity will have practical consequences. Or, to put it another way, knowing and understanding God as Trinity is going to impact our everyday Christian lives.

The great Scottish preacher James S. Stewart made the point best when he asked his congregation, "Is it not true that you cannot say all that is contained for you in the word 'God' until you have said Father, Son and Holy Spirit? That is to believe the Trinity."[4]

Why Trinity? Answer: It is the only way to make sense of the facts. I like what C.S. Lewis said in one of his radio broadcasts on the Trinity, later published in his book, *Mere Christianity*:

> If Christianity was something we were making up, of course we could make it easier. But it is not. We cannot compete in simplicity with people who are inventing religions. How could we? We are dealing with fact. Of course anyone can be simple if he does not have any facts to bother about.[5]

So what are the facts? The basic fact is Jesus himself, as we have already seen. But there are other facts scattered throughout the record of God's self-revelation. And one of those facts is that the word "Trinity" does not appear in the Bible, the word having been coined by a church theologian named Tertullian in the third century. Before him people were using the terms such as "monad" and "triad" to describe God's nature. Because both terms carried ideas that were not biblical, Tertullian (a lay person, by the way) coined a new word—*Trinity*—to describe the three-foldness of God's nature.

And he did it to make sense of the facts before the Church. That is what the early Church was doing in all its theological debates—simply trying to make sense of the facts. Some people in our day have suggested that the church fathers took the Christian faith "off track" by forcing Greek ideas on the Bible which may or may not have been consistent with the views of the biblical writers. Some of them are guilty as charged. But not all. Most of them, like believers in any age, were seeking to communicate the good news in the words and thought forms of their contemporaries. And they did it with great care. They wanted their friends (and enemies) to come to a living faith in Jesus Christ.

One thing that helped me to embrace the work of the early church was learning about the life and theology of St. Ephrem, who lived in Syria during the time church leaders in Greece and Rome were formulating the doctrine of the Trinity. Though he was far removed from the work of Tertullian, Athanasius, Basil, and others one often reads about in books about the Trinity, St. Ephrem came to remarkably similar conclusions about the triune nature of God. As historian Sebastian Brock notes in his book on Ephrem, "in language, in modes of expression, and in thought patterns, he is nonetheless essentially one with them in his understanding of the mystery of the Trinity and the Incarnation."[6] The wrestling, searching, and "theologizing" that was going on in Greece and Rome was also going on in Syria; what was happening in Europe was happening in Asia.

So although the word *Trinity* does not appear in Scripture, the reality the early church attempted to express by the word *Trinity* does. There are throughout both the Old and New Testaments what we might call traces or "tracks" of three-fold-ness. Want to know how to get to the doctrine of the Trinity? Simply retrace the steps of the early church: turn to the biblical facts and examine these tracks of three-fold-ness.

Look first in the Old Testament at Deuteronomy 6:4. Here we find the fundamental creed of Israel: "Hear, O Israel! Yahweh is our God, Yahweh is one" (in most English translations of the Bible, Yahweh—which means something like "I am who I am"—is translated as LORD).You may remember that Jesus recited this creed in a dialogue with one of the scribes.

> One of the teachers of the law came and heard them debating. Noticing that Jesus had given them a good answer, he asked him, "Of all the commandments, which is the most important?"
>
> "The most important one," answered Jesus, "is this: "Hear, O Israel, the LORD our God, the LORD is one. Love the LORD your God with all your heart and with all your soul and with all your mind and with all your strength."

So "Yahweh is one." We are agreed on that. The real question is what is meant by the word "one"? Rather than solitary, monolithic, numerical oneness, the word "one" is seldom used in the Bible as a digit.[7] Instead, it usually means "once-for-all," "unique," "only," "only one," or "unitary."

Thus Tertullian argued that from all eternity *God is one*, but *God is not alone.*

And we find evidence of this throughout the Old Testament. It is there in the very first verse of the Bible, Genesis 1:1— "In the beginning, God created the heavens and the earth...." The Hebrew word for God in this passage is *Elohim*. Elohim is a plural noun, but it is always used with the singular form of the verbs which describe Elohim's actions. Plural noun, singular verb. This is in itself suggests some sort of plurality in the one God, but what is truly striking is Genesis 1:26, where God says, "Let *us* make humanity in *our* image, according to *our* likeness." (My italics. Note the personal pronouns—*us* and *our*—are plural).

Now it is true that the "us" could simply be a case of the so-called "royal we" by which kings and queens of the ancient near east sometimes spoke of themselves. But as far as we know there are no examples of the "royal we" in the Bible. Others have suggested that the "us" in Genesis 1:26 refers to the angelic hosts which surround God's throne. That may be a more probable explanation, except for one problem: nowhere does Scripture say that humans were created in the image of angels! Scripture says we were created in *God's* image. It seems then that the "us" must refer to God himself.

Consider another trace of three-fold-ness in Psalm 24: 9-10:

> Lift up your heads, O gates...
>> That the King of glory may come in.
>> Who is this King of glory?
>> Yahweh of hosts
>> He is the King of glory.

Here the living God is called "Lord of hosts," "Yahweh of hosts." Some scholars now argue that the phrase should be translated "Yahweh *who is* hosts," suggesting that there is within the One Lord an inherent multiplicity, a "community."[8]

Another fact pervades the Old Testament revelation of God. It is the mysterious personality called the "Angel of the Lord." We first meet this personality in Genesis 16. He appears to Hagar, the handmaiden of Sarah, Abraham's wife. But interestingly enough when she encounters this "Angel of the Lord," she concludes that she has seen God (Gen. 16:13). He appears again at the burning bush, the event recorded in Exodus 3. And the curious thing is that the text begins with the "Angel of the Lord" and then slips into referring to the Lord himself. The text says "and Moses was afraid to look at God" (Exod. 3:6). Somehow the encounter with the "Angel of the Lord" is an encounter with the Lord who is "one."

Consider also a perplexing event recorded in Genesis 18. Just before the destruction of Sodom and Gomorrah, the text says that Yahweh appeared to Abraham (Gen. 18:1).

And in the next verse the text says, "When Abraham lifted up his eyes and looked, behold, three men were standing opposite him" (Gen. 18:2). In the ensuing conversation, plural and singular alternate strangely, and in verse 13 the speaker is Yahweh. Then the "men" later identified as "two angels" set out for Sodom, but Abraham is left talking with Yahweh.[9] Early Christian preachers who saw the three Persons of the Trinity here were probably reading into the text, but this encounter does suggest some sort of "plurality" to the nature of the one LORD.

Consider more tracks in the Old Testament. We read of God's *Word*, God's *wisdom*, God's *glory*, and God's *name*. Each of these realities seems to be a personified extension of God, distinct from God and yet somehow God relating to his people. This is most clearly seen in the texts which speak of God's Spirit.

Think of Genesis 1 where God created the universe "and the Spirit of God hovered over the surface of the deep." Another example might be Isaiah 63, where God's saving actions toward Israel are ascribed to God and to God's Spirit interchangeably:

> In all their distress he too was distressed, and the angel of his presence saved them. In his love and mercy he redeemed them; he lifted them up and carried them all the days of old.
>
> Yet they rebelled and grieved his Holy Spirit. So he turned and became their enemy and he himself fought against them.
>
> Then his people recalled the days of old, the days of

Moses and his people—where is he who brought them through the sea, with the shepherd of his flock? Where is he who set his Holy Spirit among them, who sent his glorious arm of power to be at Moses' right hand, who divided the waters before them, to gain for himself everlasting renown, who led them through the depths? Like a horse in open country, they did not stumble; like cattle that go down to the plain, they were given rest by the Spirit of the LORD. This is how you guided your people to make for yourself a glorious name.

The point is that when the Hebrews affirmed that God is one, they were not thinking of a solitary, monolithic, numerical oneness. Thus Tertullian went on to argue that the one God is in reality not a numerical or monadic one but a unity which is differentiated in himself.[10] The Lord who is "one" is in some way a community, a fellowship.

Perhaps this why the angelic hosts sing to the living God with the three-fold refrain, "Holy, Holy, Holy" (Isa. 6). Perhaps it is also why God commanded the priests in the Old Testament to place his name on his people with a three-fold benediction: "The Lord bless you and keep you. The Lord make his face to shine on you and be gracious to you; the Lord lift up his countenance on you and give you peace" (Num. 6:24-26). I am not suggesting the doctrine of Trinity could be constructed upon these facts alone, but they do affirm that there is a multiplicity, a plurality within the unity of God's being. In ancient Israelite religion, the oneness of God did not mean that God could not be differentiated.

This plurality within unity is more evident when we look at the traces in the New Testament. It's everywhere! Consider what is proclaimed at Jesus' conception. The angel says to Mary, "The Holy Spirit will come upon you, and the power of the Most High will overshadow you; and for that reason the holy offspring shall be called the Son of God" (Luke 1:35). Here are three Persons: (1) the Most High, (2) the Holy Spirit and (3) the Son of God.

We see the same "tracks of three-fold-ness" in Jesus' baptism in Matthew 3:16-17:

> As soon as Jesus was baptized, he went up out of the water. At that moment heaven was opened, and he saw the Spirit of God descending like a dove and lighting on him.
>
> And a voice from heaven said, "This is my Son, whom I love; with him I am well pleased."

Here we have (1) the Spirit who descends; (2) the Voice from Heaven which speaks; and (3), the Son with whom God is well pleased.

As we have already noted, throughout Jesus' earthly ministry, Jesus speaks of a relationship with a Father and a Spirit.

- He only does what he sees his Father doing (John 5:19).
- He does what he does in the power of the Holy Spirit (Luke 9:20).
- He has come to make the Father known to his disciples (John 17:12).
- He has come to baptize his disciples in and with the

Spirit (Mark 1:8, John 1:33).

And he says that when the Holy Spirit comes, even though he comes in Jesus' stead, his coming is of Jesus and of the Father as well.[9]

When the Spirit does come upon the disciples of Jesus the tracks of three-fold-ness appear with greater regularity and sharpness. Consider the following examples:

1 Peter 1:2

Christians are described as people chosen "according to the foreknowledge of God the Father, by the sanctifying work of the Spirit, that you may obey Jesus Christ and be sprinkled in his blood. Peter is saying that our identity as disciples is grounded in three-fold-ness.

Titus 3:4-6

Paul says that God, "saved us, not on the basis of deeds which we have done in righteousness, but according to God's mercy by the washing of regeneration and renewing of the Holy Spirit whom he poured out on us richly through Jesus Christ our Savior." Paul says our salvation is grounded in this three-fold-ness.

Romans 8:9-11

Paul struggles to express the wonder of new life in Jesus Christ. "You are not in the flesh but in the Spirit, if indeed the Spirit of God dwells in you. But if anyone does not have the Spirit of Christ, he does not belong to him. And if Christ is in you , though the body is dead because of sin, yet the Spirit is alive because of righteousness. But if the Spirit of him who raised Jesus from the dead dwells in you, he who raised Christ Jesus from the dead will give life to your mortal bodies through his Spirit who indwells in you.

1 Corinthians 6:13-20

Paul, writes, "The body is not for immorality, but for the Lord, and the Lord for the body. Now God has not only raised the Lord, but will also raise us up through his power. Do you not know that your bodies are members of Christ? Do you not know that your body is a temple of the Holy Spirit who is in you, whom you have from God, and you are not your own?" Paul grounds a Christian understanding of the body, Christian sexuality in the three-fold-ness of God!

1 Corinthians 12:4-6

Speaking of the gifts that are given to us in ministry, Paul writes: "There are varieties of gifts, but the same Spirit. And there are varieties of ministries, but the same Lord. And there are varieties of effects, but the same God works in all things in all persons." Christian service is grounded in the the three-fold-ness of God.

And there's more. It is in the book of Ephesians that this litany reaches a crescendo.

Ephesians 2:18

Paul speaking of the new humanity in Christ says, "through him we both—Jews and Gentiles—have one access in one Spirit to the Father."

Ephesians 2:19-22

"You are God's household, having been built upon the foundation of the apostles and prophets, Christ Jesus himself being the cornerstone, in whom the whole building, being fitted together is growing into a holy temple in the Lord; in whom you also are being built together into a dwelling of God in the Spirit."

Ephesians 4:4-6
Paul exhorts us to maintain—eagerly maintain—the unity of the church. Why? Because there is *one* Spirit, *one* Lord, *one* God and Father of us all. The church's unity and vitality is grounded in this three-fold-ness.

And then there is Paul's prayer for the believers of Ephesus:

Ephesians 3:14-16
Paul asks that God "grant you according to the riches of his glory, to be strengthened with power through his Spirit in the inner person; so that Christ may dwell in your hearts by faith...that you may be filled up to all the fullness of God." The Christian experience is Trinitarian: The Spirit in the inner person, Christ in our hearts, being filled up to the fullness of God.

We should not be surprised that the New Testament writers speak in this way. Jesus said "Go, make disciples, baptizing them in the name of the Father, and of the Son and of the Holy Spirit." By Jesus' own definition the Christian life is a relationship with one whose name is three-fold. To be a disciple is to be immersed into, and with, the three-fold-ness of the living God.

As we have seen, the church arrived at this mind-stretching faith because it was trying to make sense of the facts: (1) God's self-revelation and (2) the Christian experience. And here is what I want to stress the most: Even without all the "traces of three-fold-ness," we would probably end up with something like the doctrine of the Trinity. For what really triggered the theological process was what ordinary people experienced when they encountered Jesus Christ.

"When the disciples saw Jesus they worshipped him." If there is a scandal in the Christian faith, it lies not in the doctrine of the Trinity but in the believer's response to Jesus: *worship*. The phenomenon occurred before his post-resurrection appearance on the mountain. It began when he was just a baby in Bethlehem's stable. Tough, rugged shepherds; sophisticated, educated wise men could not help falling on their knees before the infant Jesus and adore him. Was that right to do? The phenomenon occurred after Jesus' post-resurrection appearance. It became the dominant mark of the early church's life. Around 112 A.D. the Roman governor Pliny observed that Christians gathered together early in the morning on the first day of the week to sing hymns to Christ "as if to a god."[10] Was it right for these early Christians to do that?

A week later his disciples were in the house again, and Thomas was with them. Though the doors were locked, Jesus came and stood among them and said, "Peace be with you!" Then he said to Thomas, "Put your finger here; see my hands. Reach out your hand and put it into my side. Stop doubting and believe."

Thomas said to him, "My Lord and my God!"

Then Jesus told him, "Because you have seen me, you have believed; blessed are those who have not seen and yet have believed."

John 20:26-29

Thomas falls at the feet of Jesus in worship, saying, "My Lord and my God!" If Thomas's adoration was idolatry, why did Jesus not rebuke him?

When we consider that those who could not help worshipping Jesus were Jews—strict monotheists, whose foundational creed was "Hear, O Israel, the Lord is one God"—we have to ask one very important question: What were they doing worshipping Jesus and confessing him as Lord?

It is the experience of the heart that sets in motion the grappling of the mind which leads to the doctrine of the Trinity. If Jesus of Nazareth is just another creature—even if he is the first and greatest of creatures—then worship of him is idolatry. If, however, Jesus of Nazareth is not just another creature, if he is the *Creator become creation*, then worshipping him is wholly appropriate. And once we affirm that Jesus is divine and worthy of worship, we are off and running alongside the first four centuries of the church. For the question becomes in Adolph Harnack's words, "Is the divine which has appeared on earth and reconciled humanity with God identical with the supreme divine, which rules heaven and earth, or is it a demigod?"[11]

If the answer is yes—Jesus and God are the same of the same identity—then as little children so boldly ask, "Are there two gods?" "Of course not," we say. "Then, mommy, who was ruling the universe when God was sleeping in the arms of the Virgin Mary? Who was God praying to in the Garden of Gethsemane? Did God die on the cross?"

Keep asking those questions and you will, as disciples have for twenty centuries, end up in the doctrine of the Trinity, not, as the theologian Paul Jewett said, "to resolve the mystery of God's self-revelation (in Christ) but rather to protect that mystery."[12] It turns out that every attempt to understand Jesus apart from the Trinitarian understanding of God ends up in a *cul-de-sac*.

Yes, we need to focus on the simple facts of Jesus. The more we do, the more our hearts want to worship him. And the more we worship Jesus, the more we find ourselves caught up in the relationship at the center of the universe, surrounded by Father, Son and Holy Spirit.

Notes

1. This is how R. T. France captures many peoples' initial reaction to talk about the Trinity in his book, *The Living God: A Personal Look about What the Bible says about God* (Downers Grove, Ill.: InterVarsity Press, 1970).

2. Thomas Jefferson, "Letter to Timothy Pickering" quoted in Charles W. Lowry, *The Trinity and Christian Devotion* (New York: Harper, 1946) p. 6.

3. Lesslie Newbigin, *Trinitarian Faith and Today's Mission* (Richmond, Va.: John Knox Press, 1964) p. 33.

4. James S. Stewart, *The Strong Name* (New York: Charles Scribner's Sons, 1941) p. 254.

5. C.S. Lewis, *Mere Christianity* (New York: MacMillan, 1952) p. 129.

6. Sebastian Brock, *The Luminous Eye: The Spiritual World Vision of Saint Ephrem the Syrian* (Kalamazoo, Mich.: Cistercian Publications, 1985), p. 15.

7. S. Ethelbert Stauffer, entry for "eis," in Gerhard Kittel, ed., *Theological Dictionary of the New Testament*, Vol. 2 (Grand Rapids: Eerdmans, 1964) p. 434.

8. G.A.F. Knight, *A Biblical Approach to the Doctrine of the Trinity,* quoted in R. T. France, *The Living God: A Personal Look about What the Bible says about God* (Downers Grove, Ill.: InterVarsity Press, 1970).

9. France, *The Living God*, p. 105.

10. "Pliny's Epistle to Trajan," in *The Works of Josephus* trans. by William Whiston (Peabody, Mass.: Hendrickson, 1987).

11. Adolf Harnack, *What is Christianity?* (New York: Harper Torchbooks, 1957) p. 124. Although it is not clear that Harnack answers his own question in ways consistent with the larger Christian tradition.

12. Paul K. Jewett, *God. Creation, and Revelation: A Neo-Evangelical Theology* (Grand Rapids, Mich.: William B. Eerdmans, 1991) p. 34.

- 2 -

UNDERSTANDING
THE TRINITY

How the Church preserved the Mystery

"At the center of the universe is a relationship." That is the most fundamental truth I know. At the center of the universe is a community. It is out of that relationship that you and I were created and redeemed. And it is for that relationship that you and I were created and redeemed! And it turns out that there is a three-fold-ness to that relationship. It turns out that the community is a Trinity. The center of reality is Father, Son and Holy Spirit.

There are no two ways about it: thinking about God as Trinity is challenging. If done right, it is very invigorating. But there is no denying the fact that thinking about the one God as three and three as one is just plain hard work.

Many people see and hear the doctrine as "a riddle wrapped up inside a puzzle and buried in an enigma." The story is told of a liturgist, who on a Sunday morning was leading his congregation in the reading of the Athanasian Creed. The Athanasian Creed is the one that has phrases like, "we worship one God in Trinity, and Trinity in Unity, neither confounding the Persons, nor dividing the Substance." And phrases like, "The Father uncreated, the Son uncreated, the Holy Spirit uncreated. The Father eternal, the Son eternal, the Holy Spirit eternal." And phrases like, "The Father incomprehensible, the Son incomprehensible, the Holy Spirit incomprehensible."

After the liturgist led the reading of that line—"the Father incomprehensible, the Son incomprehensible, the Holy Spirit incomprehensible"—he was heard to mutter under his breath, "the whole thing's incomprehensible!"

Yes, thinking about God as Trinity is hard work. But it's worth it! For when we enter into the intellectual process by which the church arrived at the Trinity, we very soon discover that we are not thinking human thoughts about God; we are thinking God's thoughts about God. "Trinity" is God's way of being God. On page after page after page of the record of God's self-revelation we encounter three-fold-ness. We encounter what church historian Jaroslav Pelikan has called "footprints of the Trinity."[1]

Those who originally articulated the doctrine were ordinary disciples of Jesus—people like you and me—who were seeking to make sense of the data of God's self-revelation and of their experience of God's self-revelation in Jesus. They wanted with all their heart and mind to pray and worship and preach and evangelize in ways that were faithful to who God is.

They were monotheists, men and women who believed in one God. They passionately recited the creed "Hear, O Israel! The LORD our God, the LORD is one" (Deut. 6:4).

But they knew that something radical had taken place in the midst of history, in the life and ministry of Jesus of Nazareth, something that they could not ignore. They came to believe that in the man, Jesus, they had encountered the God who is one. "In the beginning was the Word," wrote John. "And the Word was with God, and the Word was God. And the Word became flesh and dwelt among us."

Those two texts—"the LORD is one" and "the Word became flesh"—generated a flood of challenging questions. Questions like: What is the relationship between God and the Word-who-is-God-who-has-become-flesh? What is the relationship between the divine in Jesus and the divine in the Lord who is one? And what, or *who*, is this divine reality called the Holy Spirit *with whom*, and *in whom*, Jesus baptized his disciples? What is the relationship between the Spirit and Jesus and the Spirit and the Father? The challenge was to articulate who the one God is after Christmas and Pentecost, after the coming of the Son and coming of the Spirit.

As I stated in the previous chapter, the doctrine of the Trinity is not the result of philosophical speculation carried out in ivory towers, cut off from real life. It is the result of ordinary believers trying to make sense of the facts of God's self-revelation—and trying to live in the light of those facts.

The central fact is Jesus himself. What are we to make of Jesus? Some who heard him speak picked up rocks to stone him for blasphemy. But others who heard him speak fell in love with him, and fell to their knees to worship him. Is such worship proper? Or is it idolatry? Once you say "it is proper," you start down a road, which if you stay on it, leads you to the Trinity.

We need to ask two questions. The first is, "What does it all mean?" The second is, "What does it all matter?" What does it mean to say in creed and sing in hymns "God in Three Persons, Blessed Trinity"? And then what does it matter tomorrow morning, at the office, in the classroom, at the hospital? What are the everyday consequences of knowing God is Trinity? As we proceed, I will unashamedly use the word *mystery*. The Trinitarian nature of God is a mystery. A mystery is something "which no rational argument can ultimately demonstrate and which no empirical reality can conclusively illustrate."[2] But "mystery" does not have to mean "absurdity." We may not be able to fully explain the Trinity, but that does not mean it is absurd. And conversely, just because something is a mystery is no excuse to throw up the hands and shut down the brain. We are, after all, called to love God with all our heart—and all our mind. Those who will love God with their minds, even if it gives them a headache, are those whose hearts stay on fire.

What helps me is what Dr. Paul Jewett used to tell us, his students. "The church," he said, "did not formulate the doctrine of the Trinity in order to resolve the mystery of God's self-revelation, but rather to *preserve that mystery*" (my emphasis).[3]

This suggests to me that we get at the "What does it mean?" question by asking "what does the doctrine of the Trinity preserve?"

The answer is that the doctrine preserves three basic truths which emerge from the data of God's self-revelation.[4]

1) There is one God and only one.

2) This God not only exists, but exists eternally in three distinct persons. (Theologians would say "not only exists, but subsists." I will try to unpack what this means below.)

3) The three persons are equally divine in essence and attributes.

The trick is to hold these three truths simultaneously. Most heresies result from affirming two of the truths while ignoring or denying the third.

Dr. Roger Nicole of Gordon-Conwell Seminary in Massachusetts has come up with a helpful way to diagram the preserving function of the doctrine of the Trinity.

Fig. 1

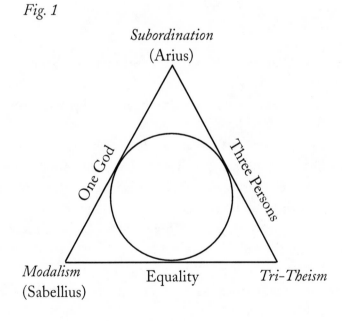

Project yourself into the center of the triangle and circle. You will remain inside the circle as long as you hold on to all three sides of the triangle. If you only hold on to two sides, you will slide into the corner where the two legs meet, and will find yourself outside the circle.

Let the circle represent the mystery of the Trinitarian nature of God. If you hold on to all three truths—God is one, but eternally subsists in three distinct persons, the three persons are equally God—you will preserve the mystery of the Triune God. But hold on to only two of the three truths and you will end up in an un-biblical view of God, a view of God which does not square with the data of God's self-revelation.

Now let's be more specific:

Modalism

Affirm that there is one God, and that the Father, Son and Holy Spirit are equally divine. But deny that God eternally exists in three distinct persons, and you end up in the corner of what is called modalism.

This heresy was first associated with a man named Sabellius, who still rears his head in our day under different names. Sabellius affirmed that Jesus Christ is fully God, but that Jesus was only a certain manifestation of the one God, a "mode of appearing." Hence the term *modalism*. Sabellius argued that the one God has revealed himself in successive manifestations: first in Old Testament times as Father, in New Testament times as Son, and in the church era as Spirit. But God is not eternally God in three persons. God just comes to us at different times in different modes.

Subordinationism

If you affirm that there is one God, and that there are three distinct persons in the Godhead, but deny that the three persons are equally divine, you will end up in the corner called *subordinationism*. This position holds that the Father is inherently divine; but the Son and Spirit possess a subordinate kind of divinity.

This heresy was first associated with a man named Arius, who also rears his head in our time under different names. Unlike Sabellius, Arius denied that Jesus is fully God. Jesus is the incarnation of the pre-existing Son of God; but the pre-existing Son of God has not eternally existed. Arius argued that the Son was the Father's first creation, and the One through whom God created everything else.

But the Son is not divine in the same sense as the Father is. Arius was famous for the line, "there was a time when the Son was not." Which, as his opponents pointed out, meant that there was a time when the Father was not the Father. In this scheme the Holy Spirit is simply an impersonal divine power. Both Sabellius and Arius wanted to preserve the oneness of God, while affirming some sort of three-fold-ness.

But Sabellius preserved the oneness by treating the three-fold-ness as "modes of appearing," while Arius preserved the oneness by relegating the Son and the Spirit to less than full divinity. Neither position won the day because neither squared with the fact of Jesus Christ as he is presented to us in the New Testament.

Tri-theism

What happens when we do not hold all three truths simultaneously? If you affirm that God exists in three distinct persons and that the three persons are equally divine, but then do not preserve the oneness of God, you will end up in the corner called "Tri-theism." Although this heresy never gained an official status it surfaces more often than we care to admit. Most popular teaching on the Trinity comes out in the end looking like there are three Gods.

There is only one way to stay out of the corners and in the circle: hold on to all three legs of the triangle simultaneously. The imagery itself reflects just how challenging the task is— I only have two hands! But if we want to know God as God has revealed God's self to be, we need to affirm— simultaneously—that God is one, God eternally subsists in three distinct person, and that the three persons are equally divine in essence and attributes.

What also makes the task so difficult is that there are no adequate analogies from nature or from the human experience. Nearly every analogy I have heard used to illustrate the Trinity illustrates what is in the corners, not what is in the circle!

Take water, for instance. Water can exist in three different states: solid, liquid, vapor. So we say, "There is an example from nature of one being three, three being one." But the fact of the matter is when applied to the three-ness of God, the analogy illustrates modalism: the same reality manifests itself in different modes under different conditions. "Ah!" say the chemistry students among us, at the so-called "triple point," at .0098 degree centigrade, 4.579 mm pressure, water can exist simultaneously as ice, liquid and gas. Such a phenomenon can help us believe that the mystery of the Trinity is not an absurdity. But what the triple-point phenomenon illustrates is "tri-theism": for at the triple point three different molecules exist in three different states.

The frustration we have in finding analogies simply reminds us that the Trinitarian nature of God is not something for which there are adequate analogies. The Trinitarian nature cannot be deduced from nature. Rather, it is something which can only be revealed from outside our experience. The doctrine of the Trinity is grounded not in nature but in God's self-revelation.

So in the rest of this chapter let's try to hold on to all three sides of the triangle—one God, three Persons, equally divine—and explore the mystery within the circle.

In 1981 I was attending a Presbyterian meeting held at St. Paul's Presbyterian Church in Los Angeles. During the meeting my mind wandered off to the stained glass windows in the sanctuary. In one of the windows was a diagram that faithfully preserved the mystery (see fig. 2 on next page). This diagram belongs inside the circle of the other diagram.

Notice the "is" and "is not." The Father is God, the Son is God, the Spirit is God. But the Father is not the Son, the Son is not the Father; the Son is not the Spirit, the Spirit is not the Son; and the Spirit is not the Father, the Father is not the Spirit. God is one in his essential being, one in substance. But in this one essential being there eternally subsist, three Persons. Stay with me—this subtle language leads us into the heart of God.

From the beginning, the church recognized that the word *person* was less than the perfect word. Our English word "person" comes from the Latin word *persona*. The Eastern church theologians shied away from it because it meant "face" or "countenance" or even "mask," the face with which an actor appears in a play. They feared, rightfully so, that the word might suggest Modalism, that the Father, Son and Holy Spirit were not eternal distinctions in the Godhead but simply modes of appearing. In our day many theologians also shy away from "person" because, to most

Fig. 2

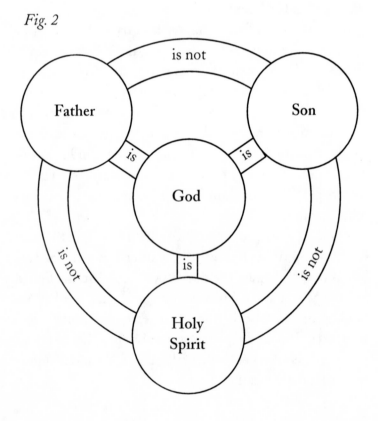

people today, the word "person" denotes an isolated, independent individual. Theologians fear the word might suggest Tri-theism.

Yet the early church theologians kept the less than perfect word to preserve the fact that although "God is one" God is not alone. There is within the one God a personal "I-thou-ness." Before the universe came into being, God could speak and someone heard and spoke back. "Persons" preserves this "I-Thou" and "Thou-I" conversation. "Persons" preserves the "*us*-ness" of God's self-revelation. The three Persons are not parts of God, nor are they mere attributes of God. Here is how the church came to put it: the three Persons are not distinctions *of* God's being; they are distinctions *in* God's being.[5]

Thus the word *subsist*. The three Persons subsist in the one Divine essence. They do not *co-exist* alongside one another. Water co-exists as liquid, solid, vapor; but it does not subsist as liquid, solid, vapor. I co-exist with my wife Sharon and our kids; but I subsist as husband, father, brother, son, pastor, teacher. The three Persons of the Trinity do not exist along side one another, but subsist in eternal inter-relatedness. Then what is it that makes for the three-ness?

We come now to the most difficult aspect of the doctrine of the Trinity. What is it that makes each of the the three persons a Person? Thomas Aquinas defined a divine Person in contrast to a human person as "an incommunicable subsistence in the divine essence." You will encounter that phrase in any book you read on the Trinity. John Calvin also used the phrase. Aquinas and Calvin used the phrase to say that while the divine Persons are distinct as Persons, not separate as individuals, yet, there is something unique, something "incommunicable" to each Person, to each subsistence in the one essence. Hold on. We're pressing in!

What then is the "incommunicable" reality whereby each Person of the One God is distinguished from the others? Again Thomas Aquinas leads the way. He says the answer lies in the way the Persons are related to one another. And the relations have to do with the source of the Persons.

The "source" of the Persons? What does that mean? The Nicene Creed gives the answer.

> We believe in Jesus Christ,
> the only begotten Son of God,
> begotten of the Father before all worlds.
> We believe in the Holy Spirit, the Lord,
> the Giver of life, who proceeds from the Father
> and the Son …

Notice the terms "begotten" and "proceeds." Those words explain the uniqueness of each of the Persons of the Trinity. As Paul Jewett explains: "The first Person is uniquely the Father in that he, and only he, is begotten of none and proceeds from none; the second Person is uniquely the Son in that he, and only he, is begotten of the Father; the third person is uniquely the Spirit in that he, and only he, proceeds from the Father and the Son."[6] The Father is the first Person of the Trinity not because he is before the Second and Third in time, but because he is the source of the distinction we call Son or Spirit.

And here is the crucial affirmation about the verbs "begotten" and "proceeds." The Father has been the source of the personal distinction eternally . . . eternally. That is, the Son is eternally begotten of the Father; the Spirit eternally proceeds from the Father and the Son.

Here is where C.S. Lewis helps us. In one of his radio talks on the Trinity, Lewis made this observation.

> We don't use the words 'begetting' or 'begotten' much in modern English, but everyone knows what they mean. To beget is to become the father of; to create is to make. And the difference is this. When you beget, you beget something of the same kind as yourself. A human begets human babies, a beaver begets little beavers, and a bird begets eggs which turn into little birds. But when you make, you make something of a different kind from yourself. A bird makes a nest, a beaver builds a dam, a human makes a radio; or he may make something more like himself than a radio; say, a statue.[7]

The distinction between "beget" and "create" is a huge one. For, as Lewis goes on, "What God creates is not God; just as what humans create is not human. What God begets is God; just as what humans beget is human." That is why "the one begotten Son of God" is God!

Now, whereas you and I are begotten by our parents in time, God the Son is eternally begotten by God the Father. As the Apostle John says in John 1:18, the Word (the Son) has always been the only begotten God who is eternally in the bosom of the Father. "Incommunicable property" of the Second Person: "eternally begotten."

This eternality of the Son is also true of the Spirit. The "incommunicable property" of the Third Person of the Trinity is his "eternal procession." Like "beget," "process" does not mean create. What God creates is not God. What proceeds from God *is* God. The universe is not a procession out of God, it is a creative work of God—something which is not himself. "Procession" (or "effusion" as some put it) is a divine "breathing." The Father and the Son eternally "breathe," and that breath is the Spirit. Is it any surprise that the Bible's word for Holy Spirit literally means "breath" or "wind"? God the Holy Spirit is, from all eternity, the life breath of God the Father and God the Son.

St. Augustine (in the third century) spent his whole Christian life reflecting on the Trinity. Talk about loving God with all your mind! And Augustine came to understand the three subsistences of the one essence in terms of love. The Father loves the Son, and the Son loves the Father. And, according to Augustine, the bond of love between the Father and the Son is the Spirit.

Again, C.S. Lewis helps us from another of his radio talks on the Trinity.

> The union between the Father and Son is such a live concrete thing that this union itself is also a Person. I know this is almost inconceivable, but look at it thus. You know that among human beings, when they get together in a family, or a club, or a trade union, people talk about the 'Spirit' of that family, or club, or trade union. They talk about its 'Spirit' because the individual members, when they are together, do really develop particular ways of

talking and behaving which they would not have if they were apart. It is as if a sort of communal personality comes into existence. Of course, it is not a real person; it is only rather like a person. But that is just one of the differences between God and us. What grows out of the joint life of the Father and Son is a real Person, is in fact the Third of the three Persons who are God.[8]

And now we are at the center of the circle. We are as close as we can get in human words. Holding on to all three legs of the triangle we stand in the mystery. The living God is one in his essential being. But in this one essential being there eternally subsist three distinct persons. The distinction lies in the relations. The Father is of no-one, neither begotten nor proceeding; the Son is eternally begotten of the Father; and the Spirit eternally proceeds from the Father and the Son.

What does it all mean? It means that in the deepest mystery of his being God is an intimate relationship, a fellowship, a community of love.

What does all this mean for us human beings? It is in that three-fold subsistence of love that we "live and move and have our being" (Acts 17:28). It is out of that love that God the Father created the world (and us in it) through the agency of the Son and energy of the Spirit. It is out of that love that God the Father sent the Son into the world to be born of the Virgin through the power of the Spirit. It is out of that love that God the Father handed over the Son, through the Spirit, to the cross, reconciling the world to himself. It is out of that love that God the Father sends the

Spirit in the name of the Son to dwell within those whom the Son purchased for the Father. From our creation, to our redemption, to our glorification, we participate in God's Trinitarian love.

Let me suggest just three everyday consequences of knowing all this. There are more which I'll spell out in the subsequent chapters.

(1) First, we now know why when *relationships* go sour, all of life goes sour. We were created in the image and likeness of God. "Let us make humanity in our image, according to our likeness" (Gen. 1:26). There are many dimensions of God's character we were created to reflect. But chief among them is this "*us*-ness" of God. God does not exist alone; and neither do we who are created in God's image. Thus God says of Adam in the garden, "it is not good for the man to be alone" (Gen. 2:18). Why? Because Adam will be lonely, yes. But more importantly because "Adam alone" is not Adam in the image of God. God is not a solitary God. Adam does not reflect who God is until Adam shares life with Eve. The singer Barbra Streisand used to sing, "People, people who need people, are the luckiest people in the world." Well, they are not only the luckiest, they are the only people who reflect the nature and character of God. Thus, after God says, "Let us make humanity in our image," the text says, "And God created man in his image: male and female he created them" (1:27).

"To be is to be related."[9] Because it is true of God; it has to be true of us. We need to be in relationship in order to be fully human. In the famous words of the poet John Donne: "No man is an island."[10] It is because we are created in the image of the Trinity that loneliness is so crushing, that broken relationships are so debilitating, that death is so painful. Lack or loss of relationship violates our essential nature, created to reflect the relational essence of God.

That is why Jesus emphasized "righteousness" so much. Righteousness simply means "right relationship." He came to reconcile us to the Father, and he came to reconcile us to each other and to ourselves. Nothing grieves the Triune God more than people who will not work at relationships. On the other hand, those who in their personal, church, business and political lives strive for righteousness are most in touch with the Trinity.

(2) Second consequence: *balance*. The Christian life, since it is grounded in and shaped by the Trinity, is like a three-legged stool. Knock out one leg and the stool wobbles. and falls. Knock out two legs and the stool falls. Most believers are Unitarian in practice. Some are binitarian. Few are truly and fully Trinitarian. We therefore live "off balance."

The God who has claimed us for himself is Father, Son and Holy Spirit; not just Father, not just Son, not just Spirit. God is God *for us*—Father. God is God *with us*—Son. God is God *in us*—Spirit. Jesus says, "Go, make disciples, baptizing them in the Name of the Father and of the Son and of the Holy Spirit." Being a disciple of Jesus, therefore, involves entering into the full reality of God's name, enjoying the full benefits of God's mighty acts as Father, Son and Spirit. Embrace the full Trinitarian nature of God and our lives have balance.

(3) Third consequence: *fullness*. "Baptizing them in the

name..." The Greek word *baptizo* means to immerse, to plunge in and beneath, to be inundated and drenched. To be baptized in the Trinitarian Name is to be immersed not just in water but in the very reality of the Name! We are given the unspeakable privilege of entering into and participating in the Trinitarian community of love!

Do you realize that? When we say "yes" to Jesus as Savior and Lord, we are immersed into the love and life of God the Father; and are immersed into the grace and truth of God the Son; and we are immersed into the power and purity of God the Spirit. Most of us are not yet experiencing and appropriating all that was given to us at conversion. We know something of the love and power of the Father. We know something of the forgiveness and freedom of the Son. We know something of the pervading and transforming glory of the Spirit. But we have yet to know the fullness available in the Triune God.

The good news is God will not rest until we do!

I am often asked to identify myself using one of the theological or ecclesiastical labels of our time. Am I Evangelical? Conservative? Reformed? Charismatic? If I must identify myself, I prefer the label "Christo-centric Trinitarian." For as I love and worship and obey Jesus Christ, I keep ending up at the feet of a Triune God. And then, all I want is all that the Father is, and wants to give me, and all that the Son is, and wants to give me, and all that the Spirit is, and wants to give me. What I want is to be alive in the intimacy at the center of the universe.

Notes

1. Jaroslav Pelikan, *The Melody of Theology: A Philosophical Dictionary* (Cambridge, Mass.: Harvard University Press, 1988) p. 138.

2. Paul K. Jewett, *God. Creation, and Revelation: A Neo-Evangelical Theology* (Grand Rapids, Mich.: William B. Eerdmans, 1991).

3. Jewett, *God, Creation and Revelation*, p.261.

4. These are modifications of propositions set forth by Dr. Roger Nicole in "The Meaning of the Trinity" in Peter Toon and James Spiceland, eds., *One God in Trinity* (Westchester, Ill.: Cornerstone Books, 1980), pp. 1-2.

5. Jewett, *God, Creation and Revelation*, p. 195.

6. Ibid., p. 275.

7. Lewis, *Mere Christianity*, p.138.

8. Ibid., p. 156.

9. John O'Donnell, *Trinity and Temporality* (New York: Oxford University Press, 1983).

10. John Donne, "meditation xvii" in *Devotions upon Emergent Occassions* (1624).

- 3 -

JOINING
THE TRINITY

Becoming Co-Lovers of God

You are wrestling with a significant issue: a decision you need to make, a relationship that needs healing, some problem at work or home, a world event, a biblical truth. You turn the issue over and over in your mind. You feel it through in your heart. And then, quite "accidentally," you pick up a book, and read in it one line that brings everything into focus. Ever happen to you?

It happened to me a few years ago. I went to the bookstore to buy a new book on the Trinity by James Torrance, a Scottish theologian. A friend who knew I was wrestling with the doctrine of the Trinity had suggested that I might enjoy the book. Because she had mentioned the book in passing, I did not remember the exact title. All I remembered was that it was by James Torrance and was on the Trinity. At the bookstore I found a copy of a book entitled *Trinitarian Perspectives* by Thomas Torrance, James Torrance's brother. "Oh, she got the Torrance brothers mixed up," I thought. "This one by Thomas must be the right book." So I bought it and went home.

Later that evening, when I had a chance to sit down to read it, I realized that it was not at all the book my friend suggested. But I decided to keep it and read it anyway. I will forever be grateful for my mistake!

I read the opening paragraph: "The doctrine of the Trinity is the central dogma of Christian theology, the fundamental grammar of our knowledge of God." Why? "Because," writes Torrance, "the doctrine of the Trinity gives expression to the fact that…God has opened himself to us."

I liked what I was reading so I read on: "…[I]n such a way that we may know him in the inner relations of his Divine Being, and have communion with him in his divine life as Father, Son and Holy Spirit."[1]

Through the reconciliation that God has worked out in Jesus Christ, says Torrance, God "has established an intimate two-way relation between himself and us and us and himself, making himself accessible to us and giving us entry into the inner fellowship of God's life."[2] Only two paragraphs into the "wrong" book, and my mind and heart were burning. Then I read, "God draws near to us"—wonderful enough! "God draws near to us in such a way as to draw us near to himself"—fantastic as well! But here is what startled me, and brought it all into focus: "God draws near to us in such a way as to draw us near to himself within the circle of his knowing of himself." I almost dropped the book! I was stunned. Tears began to flow. I wanted to both get up and dance and fall down on my knees.

That one sentence pulled together 25 years of thinking and searching and praying! No single sentence outside the

Scripture pulls it all together for me the way this one does. God, creation, incarnation, Kingdom, cross, Holy Spirit, end of history—all pulled together. "God draws near to us in such a way as to draw us near to himself within the circle of his knowing of himself."

For days and weeks I could think of nothing else. This was the gospel! The living God draws near to me, in such a way as to draw me near to himself, to draw me into the circle of his knowing of himself.

The living God is not a solitary God. The living God is not an isolated God. From all eternity the living God has lived in relationship—indeed, has lived as relationship. At the center of the universe is relationship. From all eternity the living God has been community, family. From all eternity the living God has been infinitely pleased as Father, Son and Holy Spirit.

> In the fullness of time God sent forth his Son, born of a woman, born under law, in order to redeem those who were under law, that we might receive adoption. And because you are sons and daughters, God has sent forth the Spirit of his Son into our hearts, crying "Abba! Father!"
>
> Galatians 4:4-6

> What we have seen and heard we proclaim to you also, that you also may have fellowship (*koinonia*) with us; and indeed our fellowship (*koinonia*) is with the Father, and with his Son Jesus Christ.
>
> John 1:3

The God who is "us" draws near to us, and in drawing

near to us, "us" draws us into and within the circle of his "*us*-ness," granting us entry into the inner fellowship of God's life. The community at the center of the universe draws near to me. That would be good enough. And draws near to me in such a way that the community draws me into the inner relatedness of that community. An astounding claim! But this is the fundamental message of Scripture. It is what friendship with God is all about. It is what the Kingdom is all about.

So captured was I by this great affirmation that two days later I went to the bookstore in search of the "right" book, the book by James Torrance, which I learned from another friend is entitled *Worship, Community and the Triune God of Grace*. I found it and bought it. And that evening, after things had quieted down at home, I began to read it. Marvelous! Paragraph after paragraph of pure Gospel. I kept reading until I got to page 72, where James Torrance refers to the insight of the thirteenth-century Christian philosopher John Duns Scotus. Scotus came to the conclusion that we who have been redeemed by Jesus Christ can only be called "co-lovers" with the Trinity.[4]

Again I was stunned. And again tears began to flow. "Co-lovers—that's it!" I wanted to shout out loud!

Get this: I was brought into being, and you were brought into being by the Trinity to be a co-lover within the Trinity! I was bought by the blood of Jesus Christ, and you were bought by the blood of Jesus Christ to become a co-lover with him and his Father and his Spirit!

The Bible says that "God is love" (1 John 4:8). Love implies relationship. The mystery is that long before any human being came into the picture God was already love. God had already existed as a community of love. The Father loved the Son, the Son loved the Father, and the love between the Father and the Son was embodied in the Spirit. As St. Augustine of the fourth century put it, "God is (at once) Lover, Beloved, and Love itself."[5] God is the One that loves, the One that is loved, and the Love itself.

And here is the Gospel: The God who is love draws near to *me*, a sinful, mere mortal, to draw *me* near to himself, in order to draw *me* within the circle of Lover, Beloved and Love itself. I become a co-lover with God! It is the very reason for my existence. And for yours. And for every other person who lives or has ever lived on this planet.

The living God, as the Trinitarian God, is an infinitely content God. God is not isolated. God is not needy. God is not missing anything. Yet, because the love of the Lover and Beloved cannot be contained, God creates us to be co-lovers with him. That is, God expands the circle to include us mere mortals within the circle of his knowing of himself.

And when we human beings foolishly turned away from this purpose of our existence to strike out on our own, God did not give up. The Father "so loved the world," and in the fullness of time he sent the Son to deal with our foolishness and rebellion and sin on a cross (John 3:16). The Son became one of us in order to redeem us and free us so that we could be adopted into the family at the center of the universe as real sons and daughters. And as real sons and daughters in the family, we, like the eternal Son, get filled with the Spirit, who moves us to, like the Son, cry out, "Oh Abba!"

Since those two nights in February, it has been hard to

think about anything else. I have come to see everything in light of our being created and redeemed to be co-lovers within the circle of the love of the Trinity.

My prayer has been, in the words of Thomas Benson Pollock,

Love that caused us first to be,
    Love that bled upon the tree,
Love that draws us lovingly:
    We beseech you, hear us.
Fulfill your desire for me.
    Your love, hear my cry to be a passionate
and faithful co-lover.[6]

As I have been reflecting on this, I have come to see that we are co-lovers in three ways. We are co-lovers with God *of God*; we are co-lovers with God *of one another*; we are co-lovers with God *of the world*.

As disciples of Christ, we are co-lovers with God of God.

It's a staggering thought: we are created and redeemed to enter into the love each person of the Trinity has for the other. I am created and redeemed to love each person of the Trinity with my love. That's the great commandment: "You shall love the Lord your God with all your heart, soul, mind and strength" (Matt. 22:37). But the really glorious thing is that I am invited to now love each person of the Trinity with the love of the other persons of the Trinity.

The Father really loves the Son—an understatement. The Son has been and always will be the Father's great delight. The Father draws near to us to draw us into his love for the Son! Glory! I love Jesus Christ the Son, but my love is so puny, especially compared to the Father's love for Jesus. "This is my beloved Son with whom I am well pleased" (Matt. 3:17). And the Father draws near to me to draw me near to himself so I can love the Son the way he does.

The Son really loves the Father—another understatement. This is the secret of Jesus' existence, the driving force of his ministry. He really loves the Father; this is why he is always telling us about the Father. And the Son draws near to me in order to draw me to himself so I can love the Father the way he does.

And the Spirit? The Spirit is totally taken up with the goodness and beauty of the Son and the Father. And the Spirit falls upon us—a bit stronger than draws near— so we can be ravaged with his love for the Son and Father.

Co-lovers with God of God—this is what worship is all about. The Father praises the Son; the Son worships the Father. As Hebrews 2:12 has the Son say, "In the midst of the congregation I will sing your praise." The Father draws near to us to draw us near to himself so we can praise the Son the way he does. The Son draws near to us to draw us near to himself so we can worship the Father the way he does. And the Spirit? The Spirit comes upon us to fill us with his passion to see the Father and Son glorified. The Spirit gives us entry into the inter-Trinitarian delight. This lifts a huge burden off my soul. I so often feel terrible that I am not offering the worship God is worthy to receive. My worship is so inadequate and so fickle. What I am learning is that God is receiving the worship that God is worthy to receive. The Father is receiving it from the Son; the Son is receiving it from the Father. And I am invited—I am drawn by the Spirit—into that altogether worthy worship! God is being glorified quite well, thank you. God being rightly glorified is not my burden. It is happening—and you and I are being moved by the Spirit to enter into it.

The Father trusts the Son so much that he gave him the weight of the grand enterprise of salvation. And the Son trusts the Father so much that he went to the cross knowing it was the way to accomplish salvation. The Father draws near to me to draw me into his trust in the Son; the Son draws near to me to draw me into his trust in the Father.

This, by the way, is what Jesus is referring to when he calls us to take up his yoke (Matt. 11:28–30). Yes, "yoke" is a common idiom for work. And yes, some used it to refer to the Torah, the Law of God. And yes, some argue that Jesus uses the metaphor to speak of his new Torah, his new Law as developed in the sermon on the Mount (see Matt. 5:7). But from the context of Matthew 11 we see that Jesus' yoke is his relationship with his Father. Jesus is speaking to the Father. He is praising the Father (even though his preaching is being rejected). He is speaking about no one knowing the Father except the Son, and no one knowing the Son except the Father. That is, Jesus is praying. And as he prays he turns toward his disciples and says "come to me, take up my yoke." *My* yoke. Something he himself wears. As it turns out, he has worn it from all eternity. He wore it during the days of his flesh on earth. He wears it even now.

So his yoke is his relationship with his Father; relationship of affection and trust and intimacy. And—

wonder of wonders—he calls us to enter into that relationship with him: "Take my yoke upon you."

Another way to say it is that Jesus comes to free us for adoption—to become his real brothers and sisters in his relationship with the Father. We are not just foster children, as good as that can be. We are legally adopted, with the same rights and privileges of the only-begotten Son. I find myself shaking my head in wonder many times a day!

As disciples of Christ, we are co-lovers with God of one another.

We are drawn into the inner knowing of the Trinity together. How can we but love one another? How can we stand or sit or be within the circle of God's knowing of himself and not learn to love one another?

As an adopted child of God, you have become to me like Jesus, my elder brother. As I look at him, I cannot but see you held by him in his love. As you look at him, you cannot but see me held by him in his love. I am ashamed that I have come to understand this so late in my life, but at least it is happening! I cannot think of anyone without seeing them within the circle of the Trinity.

And this lifts a huge load off my soul as well. I am commanded to love you as I love myself, right? And you are commanded to love me as you love yourself, right? Sometimes I can do it, but more often than not, I can't.

As a disciple of Jesus, I am commanded to love you as he loves you. And you are commanded to love me as he loves me. If we obeyed him it would change the world, let alone the church. Sometimes I can do it, but more often than not, I can't.

But here's what I am learning: I am to love you not as much as he loves, but with him as he loves you. That is, I am to see him loving you and join him in his loving you. Co-lovers with him. Co-lovers of one another!

We want you to "have fellowship with us," John says in 1 John 1:3, "and our fellowship is with the Father and his Son Jesus Christ." We do not have direct relationship with each other. Our relationship is always with each other in and with the Trinity. I am to love you by joining the Trinity loving you. You are to love me by joining the Trinity loving me.

This, by the way, is why death does not end our relationship. We are now within the circle of God's self-knowing. Death does not take us out of the circle. Death changes the way we share but not the fact that we are still there in him and with him. That is what we mean by "the communion of the saints"—communion within the Trinitarian communion, a communion that death cannot destroy. As my grandmother told me before she died, "Darrell, we can meet every day around the throne."

As disciples of Christ, we are co-lovers with God of the world.

How could it be otherwise? As Robert Boyd Munger, the author of *My Heart, Christ's Home*, used to tell his students, "the closer you get to the heart of God, the closer you get to what is on God's heart."[7] And on God's heart is the world—your neighbors and my neighbors; empty, rebellious, broken people for whom the Son died. People over whom the Spirit broods. How can we help but love them when we know and feel the love of the Trinity for them? Not just loving them with our love, temporarily, up and down. But seeing God loving them and joining God loving them. We are called to be co-lovers with God of the world.

You can see that the three great disciplines of discipleship—worship, community, mission—cannot be separated, because they are grounded in the Trinity. Co-lovers with God of God—worship. Co-lovers with God of one another—community. Co-lovers with God of the world—mission.

The living God is not a solitary God. The living God is not an isolated God. The living God is a relationship, a community, a Trinity. And this God draws near to us to draw us near to himself within the circle of his knowing and loving of himself.

And so, Dallas Willard, Professor of Philosophy at the University of Southern California, can write

It is being included in the eternal life of God that heals all wounds and allows us to stop demanding satisfaction. What really matters, of a personal nature, once it is clear that *you are included*? You have been *chosen*. *God* chose you. This is the message of the Kingdom.[8]

Notes

1. Thomas F. Torrance, *Trinitarian Perspectives: Toward Doctrinal Agreement* (Edinburgh: T. & T. Clark, 1994) p. 1.

2. Torrance, *Trinitarian Perspectives*, p. 1.

3. All biblical quotations in this chapter are taken from the New American Standard Version.

4. James B. Torrance, *Worship, Community and the Triune God of Grace* (Carlisle: Paternoster Press, 1996) p. 72.

5. St. Augustine, *De Trinitate Book X*, trans. by Edmund Hill (Brooklyn, N.Y.: New City Press, 1991).

6. Thomas Benson Pollock, quoted in Paul K. Jewett, *God, Creation, & Revelation: A Neo-Evangelical Theology* (Grand Rapids, Mich.: William B. Eerdmans, 1991) p. 306.

7. Robert Munger, *My Heart, Christ's Home* (Downers Grove, Ill.: InterVarsity Press, 1992).

8. Dallas Willard, *The Divine Conspiracy: Rediscovering Our Hidden Life* (San Francisco: Harper, 1998) p. 341.

- 4 -

ENTERING
THE TRINITY

Living in the Circle of "Us"

Here is the good news: The living God is not a solitary God. The living God is not a lonely God. The living God is the Trinitarian God. From all eternity the living God has existed in community as Community; in fellowship as Fellowship; in relationship as Relationship. From all eternity the living God has existed as Father, Son and Holy Spirit. From all eternity the living God has been able to speak of himself as "we," "us," and "our."

And here is the incredibly good, good news. We human beings were brought into being to participate with God in that *us*-ness. It is almost too good to be true! I was brought into being by the Trinity—and you were brought into being by the Trinity—to participate in the inner life of the Trinity! I was bought by the blood of Jesus Christ, the Second Person of the Trinity—you were bought by the blood of the Second Person of the Trinity—to participate with him in his communion with the First and Third Persons of the

Trinity. Because of the work of the Son on the cross, and because of the re-generating work of the Holy Spirit in our hearts, you and I who say yes to Jesus as Savior and Lord are adopted by the Father into the Trinitarian Family. We become real sons and daughters in relationship with the only begotten Son. We enter into the Only Begotten's relationship with the Father and the Holy Spirit. When we say yes, we come home.

Earlier on I shared with you a sentence from a book by the Scottish theologian Thomas Torrance. Through the coming of Jesus Christ and through the coming of the Holy Spirit, God "draws near to us in such a way as to draw us near to himself with the circle of his knowing of himself." Amazing! The book is entitled *Trinitarian Perspectives*. The sentence is on page two. No sentence outside the Scriptures has gripped my mind and heart the way this one has. "God draws near to us." That is wonderful enough, is it not? That the living God would draw near to me is enough to rejoice in the rest of life. But that's not all. "God draws near to us in such a way as to draw us near to himself." Again, that too is wonderful enough—is it not?—that the living God would come and pull me to himself. But there is more: "God draws near to us in such a way as to draw us near to himself within the circle of his knowing of himself." *Within the circle*—can you think of anything more wonderful than that? The living God, who speaks of himself as *us*, draws near to us in such a way as to draw us near to the *us* within the circle of the *us*.

That is why we were created. That is why we were redeemed. That is what it means to be saved, to be born again. It is the blessing signified in our baptism. Being immersed into water in the Trinitarian Name (Father, Son and Holy Spirit) points to our being immersed into, plunged into, the three-fold-ness of God, to participate in the Name, to participate in the inner life of the Trinity.

In his dialogue with the philosophers in Athens, the apostle Paul says about the living God, "He is not far from us; for in him we live and move and have our being" (Acts 17:27-28). In light of understanding God as Trinity, as the "us," that claim makes all the more sense. In the Community at the center of the universe we live and move and have our being. Note the preposition "in." Not just "because of"; not just "because of him we live and move and have our being." And not just "through"; not just "through him we live and move and have our being"; but *in.* The Trinity draws close to me to draw me close to the Trinity, to draw me *within* the circle of the Trinity's life of Father, Son, and Holy Spirit!

"Father, Son and Holy Spirit." Perhaps here is where I can address one of the questions being asked about Trinity-language in our time. Out of sensitivity to legitimate feminist concerns, many are asking, "can we finish a better way to speak of God's Trinitarian being?" And it is being proposed in many Christian circles, and being written into the liturgy in many Christian circles, that we should speak of the Trinitarian God as "Creator, Redeemer, Sanctifier." The proposal has some merit, for it does highlight the dominant works of each Person of the Trinity.

But, though it has some merit, it misses the mark; and, therefore, cannot replace traditional language. Why? For two reasons.

First, although the Father is Creator he is not the only Person of the Trinity who creates. The Son and the Spirit are also active in creation. Colossians 1:16—"by him (the Son) and for him (the Son) all things have been created." Recall Genesis 1:1— "and the Spirit of God was hovering over the surface of the waters." And the Son is not the only Person of the Trinity who redeems. The Father and the Holy Spirit are also active in redemption. The Father so loves the world that he sends the Son, and therefore also in some way suffers; and the Spirit is there empowering the Son to do his saving work. And the Spirit is not the only Person of the Trinity who sanctifies. The Father and the Son are also active in the work of making us Holy. The formula "Creator, Redeemer, Sanctifier," as helpful as it is, is not Trinitarian: it only says three things about the Trinity.

The formula is defective for a second, more fundamental reason. It misses the heart of God's self-revelation. The essence of the Trinity is relationship. "Creator, Redeemer, Sanctifier" is not the language of relationship. Conceivably there can be a Creator without a Redeemer or Sanctifier. But there can be no Father without a Son, and no Son without a Father. "Spirit" makes no sense unless it is the Spirit "of someone."

The way forward in knowing God as Trinity is to discover that what is meant by "Father" is not what is meant by many people's experience, especially many women's experience, of "father." Instead of changing the Father-Son language, the more faithful, and therefore, more redemptive way forward is to realize that this Father-Son relationship goes beyond the best father-son relationship any humans have forged. It goes beyond the best mother-daughter, mother-son, father-daughter relationship among humans. It is a relationship like no other.

And we were brought into being by that Relationship for that Relationship! We were bought by the blood of the Lamb to participate in that Relationship.

The God who is "*us*" draws near to us so that "*us*" can draw us into the circle of his "*us*-ness." The God who is Trinity draws near to you and me and draws you and me near to himself, so that you and I can participate in the life within the circle of the Trinity.

The question I invite you to grapple with is this: *into* what are we being drawn? That is, what is going on *within* the circle of the "us"? Or, what are the dynamics of this Relationship at the center of the universe?

The good news is the answer is not a total mystery. Mystery, yes. But not a total mystery. For the Second Person of the Trinity has come to earth and taken on our earthliness, clothing himself in our flesh and blood. And, as one of us, he lives out, in human form, the dynamics of life within the circle of God's knowing of himself. When we read the New Testament gospels we are reading the revelation of what goes on within the Trinity!

For some time I have been trying to understand and express the inner-Trinitarian dynamics. And I have come up with seven words. There are hundreds more! But seven that express the essential dynamics of the Life within the circle of the "Us."

1. The first word is *intimacy*. I could have used the word *love*. But I chose the word intimacy because it goes deeper

than what most people today mean by love. At the center of the universe is intimacy, a deep, abiding, tender, affectionate belonging. The Father really loves the Son. And the Son *really* loves the Father. And that love, that intimacy, is so real it is embodied in the Holy Spirit. This is the major thrust of the Gospel of John. In John, Jesus unfolds the intimacy of the Trinity's life, which is why my friend Earl Palmer entitled his little commentary on John, *The Intimate Gospel*.[1] Jesus reveals the rich interconnectedness he has with the Father and with the Spirit.

And Jesus tells us that it is for that intimacy we were created and redeemed. As he prays to the Father: "I in you, you in me, and they in us." All our longing is longing for this intimacy. We are all wired for intimacy. All our hungers are finally hunger for this; all our thirsts are ultimately thirsts for the passionate belongingness of God. The cry for intimacy that marks our time is unknowingly the cry for intimacy with God.

Intimacy himself draws near to us so that he can draw us within his intimacy. Praise God! This is what is meant when through the prophet Isaiah the living God says again and again, "I have created you for myself." The Holy Spirit comes upon us and moves us from the depths of our being to join the Son in crying out "Abba, Father."

2. The second word is *joy*. I could have used the word *happiness*. But I chose the word joy because it goes beyond happiness. At the center of the universe is joy. Unalloyed joy. God really enjoys being God! The Father enjoys the Son: "You are my constant delight." And the Son enjoys the Father: "In you does my soul rejoice." And that joy is so real

that it is embodied in the Holy Spirit. This too is a major thrust of the Gospel of John. Jesus does what he does out of joy. And he invites us into his joy.

John 15:11—"These things I have said to you that my joy may be in you, and that your joy may be made full."

John 16:24— "Ask, and you will receive, that your joy may be made full."

John 17:13—Jesus prays for us saying, "may they have my joy made full in themselves."

Yes, since the ruin of creation by sin, there is sorrow within the circle. No one grieves over the ruin of the world or the wreckage of human life like the living God. Yet, underneath that sorrow is the joy the Trinity has in being our Savior. The joy of coming to rescue us and heal us and re-make us.

> Joyful, joyful, we adore Thee,
> God of glory, Lord of love.
> Hearts unfold like flowers before Thee,
> opening to the sun above.
>
> Melt the clouds of sin and sadness,
> Drive the dark of doubt away.
> Giving of immortal gladness,
> Fill us with the light of day. ....
> All Thy work with joy surround Thee ....
> lift us to the Joy divine.[2]

Joy himself draws near to us to draw us within the circle of his joy. "Joy unspeakable and full of glory" as the apostle Peter put it (1 Pet. 1:8).

3. The third word is *servanthood*. Servanthood? In God? Yes, at the center of the universe is servanthood. The Father serves the Son. The Son serves the Father. And that Servanthood is so real it eternally manifests itself as the Spirit of servanthood. The circle is the circle of servanthood.

How do I know this? Because of the great hymn recorded in Philippians 2:5-11.

> Have this mind which was in Christ Jesus,
>   who because he was in the form of God
> did not consider equality with God
>   something to take advantage of,
>   but rather considered equality with God to be
>   emptying himself and taking on the form of a servant.

This early Christian hymn suggests that in his pre-earthly state the Son is contemplating what it means to be God. And it comes to the conclusion that to be like God is to be servant—which is why Jesus washes feet. "What are you doing down there on your knees washing feet, Jesus?" "I told you, I only do what I see my Father do. I am doing for you what my Father has done for me for all eternity."

The further into the circle of intimacy and joy we are drawn the freer we become to join intimacy and joy in giving themselves away. Servanthood himself draws near to us to draw us within the circle of servanthood.

4. The fourth word is *purity*. I could have used the word *holy*, but I chose purity because that is what holy is. At the center of the universe is purity. No twistedness. No deceit.

No manipulation. No dirtiness. Clean. Whole. Absolute Purity. Radiant fire, purifying everything within its circle. As John says, "God is light, and in him there is no darkness at all."

Can you handle it? Purity himself draws near to us to draw us within the circle of purity. Isaiah cries out "woe is me ... I am a man of unclean lips. I live among a people of unclean lips." Peter cries out "depart from me for I am a sinner Lord." The Trinity cries out "Do not be afraid. The Purity will not fry you. It will only burn away all that is not pure."

5. The fifth word is *power*. Of course! At the center of the universe is power. Immeasurable power. Power that makes rabbits and monkeys and deer and whales and humans. Power that effortlessly flings planets and galaxies into whirling space. Power that holds the universe together moment-by-moment.

Think about that: "Holds the universe together." I can't even hold myself together. Do you know how much the earth weighs? The best estimate is six sextillion tons: that's six followed by 21 zeros. And yet here it is "hanging" in space, perfectly balanced, rotating on its axis at roughly 1,000 miles an hour. Six sextillion tons spinning at 1,000 miles per hour! And rotating around the sun at 19 miles a second, or 1,140 per hour. And the sun. Do you realize that every square yard of the sun continually gives off 130,000 horse power of energy? That's the energy equivalent of 450 V-8 engines. How many square yards are there on the surface of the sun? Millions! The Triune God holds it all together! And to think that our sun is not the brightest or most powerful star in the universe. And to think that the sun and its system of planets is only one of 100 billion systems that make up the Milky Way. How does Isaiah put it?

> Lift up your eyes on high and see who has created these stars ... He calls them all by name; because of the greatness of his might not one of them is missing.
>
> Isaiah 40:26

Can you handle it? Power himself draws near to us to draw us within the circle of Power. Jesus tells the disciples they will be "clothed with power from on high" (Luke 24:49). Jesus promises "you will be baptized with the Holy Spirit ... all you shall receive power" (Acts 1:5, 8). The apostle Paul prays for the Ephesians that God would open the eyes of their hearts to know "the surpassing power toward us who believe" (Eph. 1:19). Power that raised the crucified Jesus from the dead. Power that seated the risen Jesus far above all rule and authority. Power that overcomes addiction. Power to endure difficult circumstances and difficult people. Power to serve with joy. Power that supremely manifests itself in being utterly powerless in giving his life life for us on a cross.

6. The sixth word is *creativity*, which follows on the heels of servanthood and power. At the center of the universe is endless creativity. Not only in calling worlds into being out of nothing. But creativity that finds a way where there seems to be no way. Like coming to earth through the womb of a virgin. Pretty creative, wouldn't you say? And by overcoming

death by letting death first overcome him; and like gaining the victory over evil by letting evil first have its way with him. And like bringing the crucified through the grave into a whole new order of existence which death cannot touch.

Rejoice! Creativity himself draws near to us to draw us within the circle of his creativity. That is what spiritual gifts are all about—the Trinitarian God sharing his creativity with us. As Paul told the Corinthians:

> There are varieties of gifts, but the same Spirit. And there are varieties of ministries, but the same Lord. And there are varieties of effects, the same God who wants all things in all persons.
>
> 1 Corinthians 12:4-6

Creativity himself draws near to us to draw us within the circle of divine creativity, releasing divine wisdom and knowledge, releasing divine prophecy and miracles, releasing divine helping and leading; enabling us to preach and paint and write poetry and make music and films; and to build bridges and cities, and teach geometry, invent computers, grow gardens; and to heal broken bodies, and more, to heal broken relationships.

Living within the circle of the Trinity we will never hear "can't do it." We belong to a creative, "can do" God, a God who finds a way where there seems to be no way.

7. The seventh word is *peace*. At the center of the universe is peace. Not because the Triune God is unaware of the chaos in the world. Not because the Trinity is out of touch with the pain of the world. It is because the Trinity is

never threatened by it all. The Trinity never panics. The Triune God is never immobilized by fear. Never worried that someone or something is going to thwart his purposes.

And Peace himself now draws near to us to draw us near to himself within the circle of his peace.

"Be still and know that I am God. I will be exalted in the earth" (Psa. 46:11). "And his Name shall be called Prince of Peace. And the government shall rest on his shoulders" (Isa. 9:6-7).

The Gospel of God as Trinity is overwhelms me. I only wish I had understood what I now understand much earlier. The living God is not a solitary God. The living God is not a lonely god. The living God is Relationship. And this God draws close to us to draw us close to himself, pulling us into the circle to participate with him in the Trinitarian Intimacy, Trinitarian Joy, Trinitarian Servanthood, Trinitarian Purity, Trinitarian Power, Trinitarian Creativity and the Trinitarian Peace.

Notes

1. Earl F. Palmer, *The Intimate Gospel* (Waco, Texas: Word, 1978).
2. Henry J. van Dyke, "Joyful, Joyful, We Adore Thee" (1907).

- 5 -

EXPERIENCING THE TRINITY

Praying the Boldest Prayer Imaginable!

A few years ago I was encouraged by an article on the front page of the *Los Angeles Times*.[1] "Missing Pieces of Cosmic Puzzle," read the headline. It was about the fact that physicists and cosmologists cannot find 99 percent of the matter that their leading theories say must exist in the universe, nor 70 percent of the energy that their leading theories say must exist.

What encouraged me was what the author wrote in the opening paragraph: "Scientists pushing into unknown territory often find themselves at a loss for words. The more mysterious the emerging landscape, the further they must reach for appropriate language to describe it." That's how it is when we are trying to describe the three-fold-ness of God: we are reaching for appropriate language.

The article went on: "Lately, physicists who study the big questions of the universe can be heard tossing around such terms as 'quintessence,' 'X dark matter,' 'smooth stuff,' 'funny energy' and 'tangled strings.'"

And so it is with God as Trinity. We have to toss around language like "one in three," "three in one," "subsist," "persons," "undivided substance," "incommunicable subsistence," "begotten," "proceeds" and other terms I have not yet used that take us even deeper, words like *homoousios* (one substance) and *perichoresis* (mutual indwelling). "The more mysterious the emerging landscape, the further they must reach for appropriate language to describe it."

How grateful I am for the hundreds and thousands of ordinary disciples of Jesus Christ—deacons, elders, pastors —who, during the first four centuries of church history, struggled with all their hearts and minds to love God by trying to articulate the mystery of God's Trinitarian being.

After reporting the ins and outs of the current wrestling within modern physics, the article in the *Los Angeles Times* ended on this note: "For the time being, the physicists will continue to speak in tongues, struggling to invent an appropriate language, sounding more like wordsmiths than scientists. Perhaps that's appropriate. The late Nobel laureate Niels Bohr, who first saw clearly into the fuzzy heart of atoms, said that physicists trying to describe the subatomic realm in everyday language were more poets than scientists."

The scientists' struggle to describe their discoveries should help us appreciate the language of Ephesians 3:14-21.

> For this reason I kneel before the Father, from whom his whole family in heaven and on earth derives its name. I pray that out of his glorious riches he may strengthen you

with power through his Spirit in your inner being, so that Christ may dwell in your hearts through faith. And I pray that you, being rooted and established in love, may have power, together with all the saints, to grasp how wide and long and high and deep is the love of Christ, and to know this love that surpasses knowledge—that you may be filled to the measure of all the fullness of God.

Now to him who is able to do immeasurably more than all we ask or imagine, according to his power that is at work within us, to him be glory in the church and in Christ Jesus throughout all generations, for ever and ever! Amen.

Here the apostle Paul does not present us with a coherent theory of the Trinity. Rather, Paul prays the Trinity. In language that soars far beyond that of the most inspired poet, the apostle prays that we *experience* the Trinity.

The prayer itself, is one long sentence in the original Greek. One long, beautifully crafted sentence in which phrase after phrase gathers "rhetorical momentum"[2] until the words crescendo into the boldest prayer anyone can ever pray.

Strictly speaking—that is, paying strict attention to Paul's grammatical constructions—the prayer is sub-divided into three sections. Each section begins with "in order that."

Section one: In order that the Father might grant you to be strengthened with power in the inner person ... and that Christ may dwell in your hearts by faith ... rooted and grounded in love.

Section two: In order that you might be empowered to comprehend the breadth, length, height and depth ... and to know the love of Christ which surpasses knowing.

Section three: In order that you might be filled up to all the fullness of God.

We can further sub-divide the prayer into six sections, or six "movements" as I prefer to call them. Six movements of the heart in prayer before the Trinity, each of them builds on the others until the whole prayer crescendos into the extravagantly huge prayer to be filled up to the fullness of God.

Before walking through the six movements, or six ways of experiencing God as Trinity, note how Ephesians 3:14-21 begins and ends. It begins and ends with a big God.

Paul begins with the cosmic Father: "I bow my knees before the Father, from whom every family in heaven and on earth derives its name." *Every family* in heaven and on earth! The Father is the one who gives life and shape to every kind of family, earthly and heavenly, which means that we discover what it means to be father by looking at him. We discover what it means to be mother by looking at him. We discover what it means to be family by looking at how he relates to the Son and the Spirit. Heavenly and earthly, all created and sustained by this Father.

And Paul begins with a Father who gives "according to the riches of his glory." "Glory" means "all that makes God be God." "Riches of his glory" implies that the essence of God is inexhaustible. When this God gives, he gives out of a well that is full and bottomless. Annie Johnson Flint captures it well in her song, "He Giveth More Grace" (1941), second verse:

When we have exhausted our store of endurance,
When our strength has failed ere that day is
   half done,
When we reach the end of our hoarded resources,
Our Father's full giving has only begun.
His love has no limit,
His grace has no measure,
His power has no boundary known unto men;
For out of his infinite riches in Jesus,
He giveth and giveth and giveth again!

That is where Paul begins his prayer. And that is where he ends his prayer, only spelled out more fully: "to him who is able to do exceeding abundantly beyond all that we ask or imagine."

Paul kneeled before a big God. Therefore he could pray big prayers. Little God, little prayers. Big God, big prayers.

Paul kneels, not the normal posture for first century Jewish-Christian praying. The more usual way to pray was to stand (see Mark 11:25; Luke 18:11, 13). Kneeling implies humility. And kneeling implies urgency. Paul on his knees reveals his passion that the Ephesians, and we, experience the fullness of life with and in the Triune God.

Let's then move through the six movements of this big prayer one at a time. Remember what the *Los Angeles Times* article said: "The more mysterious the emerging landscapes, the further they must reach for appropriate language to describe it."

(1) Movement one: I ask the Father to grant you out of the riches of his glory to be strengthened with power through his Spirit in the inner person. "Strengthened"

would be enough. But Paul does not want us to miss the point, so he says "Strengthened with power." The Greek word is *dunamis*, from which we get the English word "dynamite."

Not just any power, but the power of the Holy Spirit. The power of the Third Person of the Trinity, who in the beginning hovered over the dark nothingness and brought into being the universe. Who in the middle of history hovered over the nothingness of the Virgin's womb and brought into being Jesus of Nazareth, the God-Man. Who now goes beyond hovering over to actually dwelling within those redeemed by the God-Man.

"The Spirit in the inner person." Inner person: the term refers to the deepest recesses of our being, to the very center of one's self, to the place within us that even we ourselves have yet to explore and understand. Down there, way in there, the Holy Spirit comes to dwell. And here he breathes his supernatural power.

And it is there, in the inner person, where we need the power. Yes, we need power in our hands and in our feet and in our back. But where we really need the power is at the center of our personalities, at the core of our being.

Which Paul makes clear in his prayer for the Colossians. Colossians 1:11—"Strengthened with all power, according to his glorious might, for the attaining of all endurance and patience." *Yes, Father, that's what we need. Power to help us endure. Power to help us be patient. Strengthen with power in the inner person so, in the words of William Barclay, we can "so bear with people that their unpleasantness and maliciousness and cruelty will never drive us to bitterness, that their unteachableness will never drive us to despair, that their folly will never drive us to irritation and that their unloveliness will never alter our love."³ Bring it on, Lord! Come into my inner person with your power!*

Here is a man struggling with leaving his wife for a younger woman. He needs power deep within the inner person. Here is a woman struggling with addiction to prescription drugs. She needs power deep within the inner person. Here is a teenager filled with rage at his parents. He needs power within the inner person. Here is a pastor weary in ministry. She needs more than a sabbatical, she needs power deep within the core of her personality.

Holy Spirit come upon us. And surround us. And enfold us. And indwell us. And breathe the power at the center of the universe into the center of our being.

(2) Movement two: I ask the Father out of the riches of his glory to have Christ dwell in your hearts through faith. In one sense, "heart" is equivalent to "inner person." But in another sense, "heart" goes beyond "inner person." If "inner person" is the center, "heart" is the control center of the center. For the biblical authors, heart means more than emotions or feelings. Heart involves mind and will. Heart is the place inside us where we gather and store all the data, and where it is all sorted out, and where we decide how to react or act in light of it all.

I pray that the Father grant that Christ himself dwell at the control center of the center. Yes, Father! The Third Person of the Trinity moving deep within, the Second Person of the Trinity dwells deep within, exercising control deep within. The more mysterious the energy landscape, the further the reach for appropriate language.

"That Christ may dwell." *Dwell.* There are two words in the Greek New Testament that are rendered in English as "dwell." One (*paroikeo*) means to "inhabit as a stranger," to live as an alien away from home. The other (*katoikeo*) means to "settle down somewhere." It refers to a permanent as opposed to a temporary abode."[4] It is the second word that Paul uses in his prayer. *Father, I ask that Christ not only visit our hearts, but that he come and take up permanent residence in them.*

That is why Robert Munger entitled his book *My Heart, Christ's Home.*[5] Little book, big message. Munger calls us to take Paul seriously and to view our lives as a house. And to own the fact that Jesus Christ comes to live in it, not just as a honored guest but as a permanent resident. More than that: as the Master of the house. And Munger encourages us to open up all the rooms and closets of our house to Christ's controlling Presence. To let him go past the living room, into the dining room, into the kitchen, into the family room, into the recreation room, into the study, into the bedroom. To let Christ get his hands on the control panel in every room. *Father, I ask that your Son dwell at the very core of my personality!*

Only two movements and already things are changing!

(3). Movement three: "I ask the Father to grant you out of the riches of his glory, to have you rooted and grounded in love." In the "love of the Trinity" is what Paul means. In the love of the Father, Son and Holy Spirit. Rooted and grounded is the natural consequence of the Spirit empowering the center, and Christ controlling the center.

"Rooted and grounded." In his enthusiasm Paul has mixed metaphors. "Rooted" is an agricultural metaphor. "Grounded" is an architectural metaphor. Paul prays along both lines, asking that the love of the Trinity be the soil of our lives. And asking that the love of the Trinity be the foundation of our lives. That the roots go deep into that love so that good fruit emerges on the leaves. That the foundation goes deep into that love so that the building is strong.

We all automatically act and re-act out of the soil in which we live. The building we are constructing of our lives is determined by the kind of foundation on which we stand. *O Father, please, please may the soil and foundation of my life be the pure and strong love you and your Son share in the Spirit.*

(4). Movement four: I ask the Father to grant you out of the riches of his glory to be empowered to comprehend with all the saints what is the breadth, length, height and depth. The question is, breadth, length, height, depth of what?

Scholars suggest a number of answers. Two are most worthy of consideration.

a) The first is wisdom. *Strengthen us to grasp the breadth, length, height and depth of your wisdom.* Why this possibility? In Ephesians 1:8, wisdom is one of the spiritual blessings in the heavenly places we have been given in Christ. In Ephesians 1:17, Paul prays that we might be given "a spirit of wisdom." Then in Ephesians 3:10, Paul says that through the Church "the manifold wisdom of God" is being made known to the principalities and powers.

It is argued that in his second prayer, Paul is praying that we be given strength to comprehend God's wisdom—its breadth, length, height, depth. And there is biblical precedent for using those four words in connection with wisdom.

> Would that God would speak, and open his lips against
>   you, and show you the secrets of wisdom!
> Can you discover the depth of God?
> Can you discover the limits of the Almighty?
> They are high as the heavens, what can you do?
> Deeper than Sheol, what can you know?
> Its measure is longer than the earth and broader than
>   the sea.
>
> Job 11:5-9

> Oh, the depth of the riches both of the wisdom and knowledge of God! How unsearchable are his judgments and unfathomable his ways!
>
> Romans 11:33

b) The second possibility for breadth, length, height, depth is love. Although wisdom is likely in the back of Paul's mind, love is at the front. The reference to breadth, length, height and depth is preceded by "rooted and grounded in love" and followed by "to know the love of Christ."

O Father, help us to comprehend the breadth, length, height and depth of the Trinitarian love. How in the world —or in heaven—can we mere mortals get our minds around this love? Breadth: God's love is broad enough to encompass every tribe and tongue and nation. Broad enough to know and pursue all five billion people on the planet! Length: Long enough to encompass all of time. God's love was there in eternity past, long before we were created, long before we sinned. And God's love will be there in eternity future—inexhaustible, ever richer. Depth: God's love is deep enough to make the ever downward journey. The second Person of the Trinity becoming one of us, a real flesh and blood man. And choosing to take on our sin, to become sin. Deep enough to find me! Deep enough to reach inside me and grab my rebellious heart and win me to himself. Height: God's love is high enough to lift us out of sin and into his Trinitarian Fellowship.

> Oh the deep, deep love of Jesus,
>   vast, unmeasured, boundless, free.
> And it lifts me up to glory,
>   for it lifts me up to Thee.[6]

Paul prays that we comprehend this broad, long, deep and high love. More specifically, he prays that we "be strengthened to comprehend." Why do we need strength to comprehend? Because the word rendered "comprehend" (*katalambano*) means more than to understand. It means "lay hold of as one's own," "to seize," "to take possession." It is the word used in John 1:5: "And the light shines in the darkness and the darkness does not overcome it." Jesus the light has come to the world. The darkness tried to lay hold of it, to seize it, to take possession of it, but could not.

Oh, Father, grant us strength to seize, to take hold of the breadth, length, height, depth of your love. Overcome any resistance or fear or suspicion or laziness, and strengthen us to grasp it with our whole being. Then will we sing with the old hymn:

> Could we with ink the ocean fill,
> And were the skies of parchment made,
> Were every stalk on earth a quill,
> And every person a scribe by trade,
>
> To unite the love of God above,
> Would drain the ocean deep.
> Nor could the scroll contain the whole,
> Though stretched from sky to sky.[7]

(5) Movement five: "I ask the Father to grant you out of the riches of his glory to know the love of Christ which surpasses knowledge." To know what surpasses knowing!

The Greek word rendered "know" means more than intellectual assent. It means to know personally, to experience. To experience what surpasses experiencing! The implication being that we will never be done with knowing this love. There will always be more to know, to experience.

How do we "know" in this sense? Paul asks the Father to make this happen. Do we have a role to play? Yes, it is to open up to the Father doing it through the indwelling Son and empowering Spirit.

"May he strengthen you to know." Why this "strength to know?" The implication is that, on the one hand, there are obstacles to overcome, and on the other hand, such knowing needs resources beyond the human.

(6) Movement six: I ask the Father to grant you out of the riches of his glory to be filled up to all the fullness of

God. Glory! The verb is passive, telling us that this fully can only be done by God.

"Filled up to all the fullness of God." Extravagant language for an extravagant reality. "Filled up." The verb means to "fill to full capacity," to "fill to the brim." *Father, fill us up to the brim out of the riches of your glory, fill us to full capacity.*

And the measure of this filling is what Paul calls "the fullness of God." The *pleroma.* The sum total of all God's attributes.[8] "The fullness of God" is the sum total of God's wisdom, power, purity, grace, truth, beauty, mercy, justice, light. "The fullness of God" is all that makes God be God!

The more mysterious the emerging landscape, the greater the reach for appropriate language to describe it!

Paul is praying that we—broken, frightened, sinful, anxious, empty human beings—be filled up to the degree, to the level, to the extent that the filling can only be measured by "the sum total of God's attributes."

With what does God fill us so that the filling is measured by "the fullness of God?" Answer: the fullness of God! In Colossians 2:9, Paul says that all the fullness of Deity dwells in Christ in bodily form. And in Colossians 2:10, he says, "And in Christ, you have been made complete." In relationship with Jesus Christ, we partake of that fullness. For the Spirit involves the inner person and Christ himself makes his home in our heart.

Now, in Ephesians, Paul is clear that this filling takes place over a lifetime. In Ephesians 1:23, he calls the church "the fullness of him Who fills all in all." Then in Ephesians 4:13, he calls the church to exercise the gifts of the Spirit so we can grow up into "the fullness of Christ." And in Ephesians 5:18, he exhorts us to "keep on being filled with the Holy Spirit." His point? As we open up each room of the house, the fullness fills more until we are full of the fullness.

It is important to say at this point that "being filled up to all the fullness of God" does not make us God. Godly, yes, but not God. Filling a glass with water does not make the glass water. Filling a balloon with helium does not make the balloon helium. Filling a human being with God does not make a human being God. The filling makes a human being human—finally all we were created to be: creatures pulsating with the Presence of the Creator.

This is the good news, the Gospel. The Triune God draws near to us to draw us near to himself, pulling us within the circle of the Trinitarian relationship, in order "to occupy and possess, pervade and permeate" every part of our lives. Here is how missionary Dr. Visser't Hooft put it:

> To pray "fill us up to all the fullness of God" cannot simply mean "let us have a little bit of this fullness to make us happy." No! It means "Come Thou living God, come Thou Living Christ, and come Thou creative Spirit, Giver of life, and transform us altogether, so that we may be truly converted, radically changed."

You see, Paul's prayer pays an implicit compliment to every human being. Paul's prayer says that we were made in such a way that the only thing that finally fills us is the Triune God. And every human being has at least one thing in common with every other human being: we cheat ourselves. We try to fill ourselves with everything but the Triune God. God says through the prophet Jeremiah: "My people have committed two great sins: They have forsaken me the fountain of living water and dug for themselves cisterns, broken cisterns, that hold no water" (2:13).

I ask the Father to grant you out of the inexhaustible riches of his glory, to be strengthened with power through his Spirit in the inner person; to have Christ dwell in the control center through faith; to be rooted and grounded in the love of the Trinity; to be strengthened to apprehend the breadth, length, height and depth of the love of the Trinity; to be strengthened to experience the love of Christ which surpasses knowing; and to be filled up to the brim with all that makes God be Trinity!

This is a big prayer because we are praying to and *with* a big God who is able to do immeasurably more abundantly than all we ask or imagine.

The more mysterious the landscape becomes, the further we need to reach for appropriate language.

Notes

1. K.C. Cole, "Missing Pieces of the Cosmic Puzzle; As physicists continue pondering the nature of the universe, they say they can't find 70% of its energy, or the words to describe their problem," *The Los Angeles Times*; June 15, 1998; Record edition; p. 1.

2. Andrew T. Lincoln, *Ephesians,* Word Biblical Commentary (Waco, Texas: Word Publishing, 1990) p. 197.

3. William Barclay, *Letters to the Philippians, Colossians, and Thessalonians* (Philadelphia, Pa.: Westminster Press, 1975) p. 110.

4. John R. W. Stott, *God's New Society: the message of Ephesians* (Leicester: Inter-Varsity Press, 1979).

5. Robert Munger, *My Heart, Christ's Home* (Downers Grove, Ill.: InterVarsity Press, 1992).

6. Samuel T. Francis, "O the Deep, Deep Love of Jesus" (1875).

7. Frederick M. Lehman, "The Love of God" (1917).

8. R. Schippers, entry for "pleroma" in Kittel, Gerhard, ed., *Theological Dictionary of the New Testament*, Vol. 1 (Grand Rapids: Eerdmans, 1964) p. 740.

THE NICENE CREED
325 A.D.

I believe in one God, the Father Almighty, Maker of heaven and earth, and of all things visible and invisible.

And in one Lord Jesus Christ, the only-begotten Son of God, begotten of the Father before all worlds; God of God, Light of Light, very God of very God; begotten, not made, being of one substance with the Father, by whom all things were made.

Who, for us men for our salvation, came down from heaven, and was incarnate by the Holy Spirit of the virgin Mary, and was made man; and was crucified also for us under Pontius Pilate; He suffered and was buried; and the third day He rose again, according to the Scriptures; and ascended into heaven, and sits on the right hand of the Father; and He shall come again, with glory, to judge the quick and the dead; whose kingdom shall have no end.

And I believe in the Holy Ghost, the Lord and Giver of Life; who proceeds from the Father and the Son; who with the Father and the Son together is worshipped and glorified; who spoke by the prophets.

And I believe one holy catholic and apostolic Church. I acknowledge one baptism for the remission of sins; and I look for the resurrection of the dead, and the life of the world to come. Amen.

FOR FURTHER
READING

Recommended books
for deeper exploration of God as Trinity

Bray, Gerald. *The Doctrine of God* (Downers Grove, Ill.: InterVarsity Press, 1993).

Brown, David. *The Divine Trinity* (LaSalle, Ill.: Open Court Publishing, 1985).

Fortman, E. J. *The Triune God* (London: Hutchinson, 1972).

Grenz, Stanley J. *Theology for the People of God* (Grand Rapids, Mich.: William B. Eerdmans, 2000).

Gunton, Colin. *The One, The Three, and the Many: The Promise of Trinitarian Theology* (Cambridge: Cambridge University Press, 1993).

Kimel, Alvin F., Jr., ed. *Speaking the Christian God: The Holy Trinity and the Challenge of Feminism* (Grand Rapids, Mich.: William B. Eerdmans, 1992).

Moltmann, Jürgen. *The Trinity and the Kingdom* (New York: Harper and Row, 1981).

Torrance, James B. *Worship, Community and the Triune God of Grace* (Downers Grove, Ill.: InterVarsity Press, 1996).

Torrance, Thomas. *Trinitarian Perspectives* (Edinburgh: T. & T. Clark, 1994).

Wainwright, A. W. *The Trinity in the New Testament* (London: SPCK, 1962).

Printed in the United States
124603LV00002B/40-45/A

9 781573 832168